CLASSIC KNITS
AT HOME

Classic Knits

AT HOME

15 timeless designs to knit and keep forever

ERIKA KNIGHT

COLLECTIBLES

photography by Katya de Grunwald

POTTER
CRAFT

New York

Editorial director Jane O'Shea
Creative director Helen Lewis
Designer Claire Peters
Project editor Lisa Pendreigh
Editorial assistant Andrew Bayliss
Pattern checker Rosy Tucker
Photographer Katya de Grunwald
Photographer's assistant Amy Gwatkin
Stylist Beth Dadswell
Illustrator Bridget Bodoano
Pattern illustrator Anthony Duke
Production director Vincent Smith
Production controller Bridget Fish

EcoYoga floor mat seen on page 18 supplied by yogamatters.com

Published in the United States by
Potter Craft, an imprint of the Crown
Publishing Group, a division of Random
House, Inc., New York.

www.crownpublishing.com
www.pottercraft.com

POTTER CRAFT and
CLARKSON N. POTTER
are trademarks and
POTTER and colophon are registered
trademarks of Random House, Inc.

Originally published in Great Britain by
Quadrille Publishing Limited, London.

Library of Congress Cataloging-in-Publication
Data is available.

ISBN-13: 978-0-307-39469-9
ISBN-10: 0-307-39469-7

Printed and bound in China

10 9 8 7 6 5 4 3 2 1

First Potter Craft Edition

introduction

Classic Knits at Home is a timeless collection of knitted basics that will add sumptuous texture to any room. Each textile has been carefully considered for its hand-crafted charm, which will withstand the vagaries of fashion. Projects range from a quintessential cable knit throw in the softest cashmere blend to a practical wash mitt knitted in eco-friendly hemp, as well as a chic yoga mat and slippers for essential comfort. The range of yarns is natural, comfortable, and easy to live with: cotton, alpaca, mohair, cashmere blends, merino wool, and hemp. All the projects are worked in a universally appealing palette of ecru, stone, natural tweed, muted gray, with accents of deep red and, of course, basic black to underline the enduring allure of all the designs.

classic knits at home collection

The pattern for the circular rug begins on page 42.

The pattern for the texture throw begins on page 46.

The pattern for the stripe cushion begins on page 48.

The pattern for the plant pot covers begins on page 52.

The pattern for the yoga mat begins on page 56.

The pattern for the yoga slippers begins on page 60.

The patterns for these classic cushions begins on page 64.

The pattern for this floor cushion begins on page 70.

The pattern for this wash mitt begins on page 74.

The pattern for this cable throw begins on page 76.

The patterns for these stitch cushions begins on page 80.

The pattern for the doorstop begins on page 84.

The pattern for the lace throw begins on page 88.

The pattern for the beaded cushion begins on page 92.

The pattern for the patchwork throw begins on page 96.

the patterns

circular rug

Taking inspiration from rustic handknits, this project is a streamlined and durable floor rug. Worked in natural hemp and using the short-row technique to create the circular shape, this practical piece is adorned with a single button.

See pages 10–11

circular rug

materials

Any double-knitting-weight natural hemp yarn (**A**), such as
    Lanaknits *Hemp Natural Hemp6*, or medium-weight parcel string
    One 18 oz (500g) ball
Any double-knitting weight mercerized hemp yarn (**B**), such as
    Lanaknits *Allhemp6*
    One 3½ oz (100g) skein in black
Pair of size 7 (4.5mm) knitting needles
Size G-6 (4mm) crochet hook
Large blunt-ended yarn needle
One large 1¼ in (30mm) button

size

One size, approximately 29½ in (75cm) in diameter

gauge

17 sts and 21 rows = 4 in (10cm) over St st using size 7
    (4.5mm) needles or size necessary to obtain gauge and A.

pattern note

For the short-row shaping, when the instructions say "turn" at the
end of the row, this means that the remaining stitches are not
worked. To avoid creating a hole when turning on a knit row, work a
wrap stitch—knit as far as instructed, then slip the next stitch
purlwise onto the right-hand needle, bring the yarn to the front
between the two needles, slip the stitch back to the left-hand needle,
and take the yarn to the back between the two needles, turn, and
purl to the end of the next row.

To make rug
Using size 7 (4.5mm) needles and
A, cast on 60 sts.
Work in St st and short rows as foll:
Row 1: K all sts.
Row 2: P all sts.
Row 3: K to last 2 sts, turn (see
pattern note, page 44).
Row 4: P.
Row 5: K to last 4 sts, turn.
Row 6: P.
Cont working in short rows as set,
leaving 2 more sts unworked on
every knit row until there are no
more sts to knit.
This completes first segment of
circle.
Start again with row 1 and cont
until 8 segments have been worked.
Do not bind off sts, but join last
segment to first segment by
grafting one st from needle with
corresponding st on cast-on edge.

To finish
Weave in any loose yarn ends.
Edging
Using size G-6 (4mm) crochet hook
and B, work 2 rows of single
crochet around outer edge of rug.
Lay work out flat and gently steam.
Sew button over hole in center
of rug.

texture throw

materials

Any super-bulky-weight yarn, such as Debbie Bliss
   Cashmerino Superchunky
   Approximately forty-three 3½ oz (100g) balls
Pair of size 13 (9mm) knitting needles
Large blunt-ended yarn needle
Scraps of suede, silk, and linen fabric to trim, approximately
   ½ yd (50cm) of each
Crochet hook (any size)

size

One size, approximately 60 in x 60 in (152cm x 152cm)
Each square measures approximately 30 in x 30 in (76cm x 76cm)

gauge

9½ sts and 16 rows = 4 in (10cm) over seed st using size 13
   (9mm) needles or size necessary to obtain gauge and yarn doubled.

To make throw panels (make 4)
Using size 13 (9mm) needles and yarn doubled, cast on 69 sts.
Row 1: K1, *p1, k1, rep from * to end.
Rep last row to form seed st and cont until work measures 30 in (76cm).
Bind off.

To finish
Weave in any loose yarn ends.
Lay work out flat and gently steam.

Lay four panels out flat and arrange to form a large square, with cast-on edges along top and bottom of throw. With WS together, sew panels together using backstitch to create a raised seam on RS.

Fringe
For fringe, cut strips of fabric approximately 13 in (33cm) long and ½ in (1.5cm) wide.
Fold one strip in half, and using a crochet hook, pull loop through a stitch at top edge of throw, pull strip ends through loop, and tighten to form a knot.
Add fringe all along top and bottom edge in same way, spacing knots equally apart as shown.

See pages 12–13

stripe cushion

Worked in one piece to create a seamless design, this basic cushion pattern is perfect for a striped motif. An integral selvage edge for the button closures keeps the look neat, and minimizes the amount of sewing needed. Snaps are used for security, but then covered by buttons for added detail.

See pages 14–15

stripe cushion

materials

Any fine-weight cotton yarn, such as Rowan *Cotton Glacé*

A: Two 1¾ oz (50g) balls in ocher
B: Two 1¾ oz (50g) balls in gray
C: One 1¾ oz (50g) ball in ecru
D: Two 1¾ oz (50g) balls in black
E: One 1¾ oz (50g) ball in lime

Pair of size 3 (3.25mm) knitting needles
Five medium 1 in (25mm) buttons and five large snaps
Medium-size blunt-ended yarn needle
Pillow form to fit finished cover

size

One size, approximately 16 in x 16 in (40cm x 40cm)

gauge

23 sts and 32 rows = 4 in (10cm) over St st using size 3 (3.25mm) needles or size necessary to obtain gauge.

stripe sequence

2 rows B
2 rows C
26 rows A
4 rows C
7 rows E
1 row C
10 rows D
2 rows C
27 rows B
6 rows C
23 rows D
4 rows C
5 rows B
11 rows A

To make cushion
Using size 3 (3.25mm) needles and
B, cast on 190 sts.
Row 1 (RS): [P1, k1] twice, p1,
k to last 5 sts, [p1, k1] twice, p1.
Row 2: [K1, p1] twice, k1, p to last
5 sts, [k1, p1] twice, k1.
Rep last 2 rows using stripe
sequence above, noting that 2 rows
B have already been worked.
Bind off in patt.

To finish
Weave in any loose yarn ends.
Lay work out flat and gently steam.
Lay work WS up, then fold side
edges into center, overlapping by
about 1 in (2.5cm) so that cover
forms a 16 in (40cm) square.
Using mattress stitch, sew top
seam of cushion, including overlap
in seam. Sew bottom seam in
same way.

Sew snaps in position, starting at
center and working outward,
placing two at each side of center.
Sew buttons on top of snaps for
decoration.
Insert pillow form.

plant pot covers

Knit these stylish covers to hide pedestrian plastic planters. They are worked in natural yarns that are perfect companions for herbs, succulents, or flowers. This basic pattern can be worked in different weights and textures to fit any pot in your home.

See pages 16–17

materials

small string pot

Medium-weight parcel string
  One 44 yd (40m) ball
Pair of size 6 (4mm) knitting needles

small one-color pot

Any bulky-weight wool yarn, such as Jaeger *Extra-fine Merino Chunky*
  One 1³⁄₄ oz (50g) ball
Pair of size 10 (6mm) knitting needles

small two-color pot

Any bulky-weight yarn, such as Rowan *Scottish Tweed Chunky*
  One 3¹⁄₂ oz (100g) ball in each of two contrasting colors
Pair of size 10 (6mm) knitting needles

large two-color pot

Any aran-weight yarn, such as Rowan *Scottish Tweed Aran*
  One 3¹⁄₂ oz (100g) ball
Any fine-weight mohair yarn, such as Rowan *Kidsilk Haze*
  One ⁷⁄₈ oz (25g) ball (yarn used three strands together)
Pair of size 8 (5mm) knitting needles

large one-color pot

Any bulky-weight yarn, such as Rowan *Scottish Tweed Chunky*
  Two 3¹⁄₂ oz (100g) balls (yarn doubled)
Pair of size 10¹⁄₂ (7mm) knitting needles

all pots

Large blunt-ended yarn needle

sizes

Small—approximately 4¼ in (11cm) in diameter and 4–4¾ in (10–12cm) tall

Large*—approximately 5½ in (14cm) in diameter and 7½ in (19cm) tall

*For large pots, work figures in parentheses ( )

pattern notes

• Experiment with various yarn textures. This pattern will work with any yarn using the needle size on the yarn label. Knit a gauge swatch when plying up yarns to determine the correct needle size.

• For the small two-color pot, change to the second color after the last decrease row before base.

• For the large two-color pot, cast on loosely using three strands of fine mohair yarn held together. Work the first six rows of the pattern in stockinette stitch, change to the tweed wool yarn, and continue following the pattern.

To make plant pot covers

Using desired needles and yarn, cast on 44 sts loosely.

Beg with a k row, work 8 (14) rows in St st, ending with RS facing for next row.

Next row (RS): K4, [k2tog, k9] 3 times, k2tog, k5—*40 sts*.

Cont in St st throughout, work even for 7 (13) rows, ending with RS facing for next row.

Next row (RS): K4, [k2tog, k8] 3 times, k2tog, k4—*36 sts*.

work even for 6 (12), ending with WS facing for next row.

K next row (a WS row) to make ridge on RS for base.

Beg with a k row, work 4 rows in St st, ending with RS facing for next row.

Shape base

Row 1 (RS): [K2, k2tog] 9 times—*27 sts*.

Row 2 and every alt row: P.

Row 3: [K1, k2tog] 7 times—*18 sts*.

Row 5: [K2tog] 9 times—*9 sts*. Leave sts on needle.

To finish

Cut working yarn, leaving a long end, and thread yarn end through remaining 9 sts.

Gather sts very tightly, then sew base seam and side seam of cover using mattress stitch.

yoga mat

This luxurious yoga mat is knitted in a
natural blend of cashmere and merino
yarn; use it on top of your existing floor
mat for added comfort. Worked in a firm
woven stitch, the contrasting border is
knitted in to give a neat finish. The mat is
then fastened with a simple cotton tie and
neatly stowed away in a handmade bag
of natural linen fabric.

See pages 18–19

yoga mat

materials

yoga mat

Any super-bulky-weight wool yarn, such as Debbie Bliss
Cashmerino Superchunky
    A: Ten $3\frac{1}{2}$ oz (100g) balls in ecru
    B: Four $3\frac{1}{2}$ oz 100g) balls in black
Pair of size 11 (8mm) knitting needles
Large blunt-ended yarn needle
Approximately 1 yd (1m) of black cotton tape, 1 in (2.5cm) wide
linen bag
Approximately 1 yd (1m) of stone linen fabric
Sewing thread
Approximately $1\frac{1}{2}$ yd (1.5m) of black cotton tape, 1 in (2.5cm) wide

size

Yoga mat: One size, approximately 69 in x $23\frac{3}{4}$ in (175cm x 60cm)
Linen bag: One size, approximately $28\frac{1}{2}$ in x 10 in (72cm x 25cm)

gauge

15 sts and 24 rows = 4 in (10cm) over st patt using size 11
    (8mm) needles or size necessary to obtain gauge.

stitches

tweed stitch

Row 1 (RS): K1, *yarn to front of work between two needles,
sl 1 purlwise, yarn to back of work between two needles, k1;
rep from * to end.

Row 2: P2, *yarn to back of work between two needles, sl 1, purlwise, yarn to front of work between two needles, p1; rep from * to last st, p1.
Rep last 2 rows to form tweed st.

pattern note
When changing from one yarn color to another in a row, twist the yarns together on the wrong side to avoid making a hole.

To make yoga mat
Using size 11 (8mm) needles and B, cast on 89 sts.
Work 2 in (5cm) in tweed st, ending with RS facing for next row.
Next row (RS): Work first 8 sts in tweed st using B, join in A and k next 73 sts, then join in a second ball of B and work last 8 sts in tweed st.
Next row: Work first 8 sts in tweed st using B, next 73 sts in tweed st using A, then last 8 sts in tweed st using B.
Rep last rows (working all sts in tweed st and keeping black borders and ecru center) until work measures 67 in (170cm), ending with RS facing for next row.
Break off A and cont with B only as foll:
Next row (RS): Work 8 sts in tweed st, k next 73 sts, work last 8 sts in tweed st.
Cont in tweed st for 2 in (5cm) more.
Bind off.

To finish
Weave in any loose yarn ends on WS. Lay work out flat and gently steam. Fold cotton tape so that one end is slightly longer than the other and sew at the fold to center of one short edge of mat.
Roll up mat and tie tape ends together.

To make linen bag
Cut a piece of linen 21¼ in (53cm) by 31¼ in (78.5cm). Along the top edge of bag, fold ½ in (1cm) to WS, press, and then fold 1½ in (4cm) over and stitch in place.
With WS together, fold fabric in half lengthwise, and taking a ¼ in (6mm) seam, stitch down side edge and along bottom edge.
Turn inside out. Making sure raw edges are inside seam and taking a ⅜ in (1cm) seam, stitch side and bottom seams again to form a French seam.
Turn right-side out.
Fold remaining cotton tape in half and stitch fold to outside of bag 3½ in (8cm) below top edge.
Insert mat, gather top of bag with cotton tape and tie in a simple bow.

yoga slippers

Perfect to wear while exercising or relaxing, these little slippers are worked on two needles and are made in a luxurious and natural cashmere and merino wool blend. Knitted in basic stockinette stitch with fully-fashioned shapings on both the sole and upper for added comfort, they are finished with tonal butter-soft suede and external seam details.

See pages 20–21

materials

Any aran-weight yarn, such as Debbie Bliss *Cashmerino Aran*
  Two 1³⁄₄ oz (50g) balls
Pair each of sizes 6 (4mm) and 7 (4.5mm) knitting needles
Scrap of soft suede for soles and pull-on tabs, approximately
  6 in x 6 in (15cm x 15cm)
Sewing thread and sewing needle for sewing on suede

size

One size, to fit US sizes 6¹⁄₂–7¹⁄₂ shoe, approximately 9 in
  (23cm) long

gauge

20 sts and 28 rows = 4 in (10cm) over St st using size 7
  (4.5mm) needles or size necessary to obtain gauge.

To make left sole

Using size 7 (4.5mm) needles, cast on 5 sts.

K 1 row.

Beg with a p row and cont in St st throughout, start shaping sole as foll:

Cast on 2 sts at beg of next 4 rows —*13 sts*.

Work even until work measures 4 in (10cm) from cast-on edge, ending with RS facing for next row.

Inc row (RS): K2, M1, k to end.

Next row: P.

Rep last 2 rows until there are 17 sts. Work even until work measures 7¾ in (19.5cm) from cast-on edge, ending with RS facing for next row.

Dec row (RS): K2, k2tog, k to last 4 sts, k2tog tbl, k2.

Next row: P.

Rep last 2 rows until there are 7 sts. Bind off.

To make right sole

Work as for left sole, but work increase row as follows:

Inc row (RS): K to last 2 sts, M1, k2.

To make uppers (make 2)

Using size 7 (4.5mm) needles, cast on 9 sts.

Row 1: K3, M1, k to last 3 sts, M1, k3.

Row 2: P.

Rep last 2 rows until there are 27 sts. Work even until work measures 4¼ in (11cm) from cast-on edge, ending with RS facing for next row.

Next row (RS): K13, bind off next st, k to end.

Next row: P first 13 sts, then turn, leaving remaining sts on a st holder. Work each side separately as foll:

Next row: K3, k2tog, k to end.

Next row: P.

Rep last 2 rows once more—*11 sts*. Work even until work measures 7½ in (19cm) from cast-on edge, ending with RS facing for next row.

Next row (RS): K3, M1, k to end. Work even for 5 rows.

Rep last 6 rows twice more—*14 sts*. Bind off.

With WS of work facing, rejoin yarn to remaining 13 sts and p to end.

Next row: K to last 5 sts, k2tog tbl, k3.

Next row: P.

Rep last 2 rows once more—*11 sts*. Work even until work measures 7½ in (19cm) from cast-on edge, ending with RS facing for next row.

Next row (RS): K to last 3 sts, M1, k3.

Work even for 5 rows.

Rep last 6 rows twice more—*14 sts*. Bind off.

To finish

Weave in any loose yarn ends. Lay work out flat and gently steam.

Edging on uppers

With RS of work facing and using size 6 (4mm) needles, pick up and knit 83 sts evenly around inside edge of upper.

Bind off knitwise.

With WS together, sew bound-off ends of each sole together to form an outside seam at heel.

With WS together, pin sole to upper, easing to fit, and sew using mattress stitch.

Oval soles

Cut out two ovals from suede for sole of each slipper—one large and one small. Using sewing thread, sew large oval to ball of sole as shown, working small stitches all around. Sew small oval to heel end of slipper in same way.

Pull-on tabs

Cut two strips of suede about ⅜ in (1cm) wide and 3¼ in (8cm) long. Fold each strip in half, pin to inside back seam at heel, and sew in place with a few firm hand stitches.

If desired, make a linen bag to fit your slippers as for bag on page 59.

classic cushions

A favorite of countless designers, the Scottish check is a modern classic. Its bold graphic quality, whether on a large or small scale, gives this design its timeless appeal. So, too, the English pinstripe characterizes British culture. These two patterns are easy to knit, made here into cushions with knitted fronts and contrasting felt backs.

See pages 22–23

classic cushions

materials

houndstooth cushion

Any double-knitting-weight yarn, such as Rowan *RYC Cashsoft DK*

    A: Two 1¾ oz (50g) balls in black

    B: Two 1¾ oz (50g) balls in ecru

Pair of size 6 (4mm) knitting needles

Large blunt-ended yarn needle

Pillow form to fit finished cover

Black felt for backing, 19 in x 19 in (48cm x 48cm)

16 in (40cm) chunky black zipper

Sewing thread

for the corsage

Piece of tweed fabric to make a strip 1 in x 59 in (2.5cm x 150cm)

One medium-size button

Safety pin

striped cushion

Any double-knitting-weight yarn, such as Rowan *RYC Cashsoft DK*

    A: Two 1¾ oz (50g) balls in black

    B: One 1¾ oz (50g) ball in ecru

Pair of size 6 (4mm) needles

Large blunt-ended yarn needle

Pillow form to fit finished cover

Red felt for backing, 19 in x 19 in (48cm x 48cm)

16 in (40cm) chunky black zipper

Sewing thread

Two large buttons

size

One size, approximately 18 in x 18 in (45cm x 45cm)

gauge

22 sts and 25 rows = 4 in (10cm) over colorwork patt using size 6 (4mm) needles or size necessary to obtain gauge.

pattern notes

- The houndstooth pattern is given as both row-by-row instructions and in chart form.
- Work the houndstooth and stripe patterns using the Fair Isle technique, stranding the yarn not in use loosely across the back of the work. Do not carry the yarn over more than three stitches at a time, but weave it under and over the color being worked.

houndstooth cushion

To make cushion front

Using size 6 (4mm) needles and A, cast on 105 sts.
P 1 row.
Beg with a k row, work in St st and houndstooth patt as foll:
Row 1 (RS): K3 A, k2 B, *k8 A, k2 B; rep from * to last 10 sts, k8 A, k1 B, k1 A.
Row 2: P1 A, *p8 A, p2 B; rep from * to last 4 sts, p4 A.

Row 3: K1 A, *k5 B, k1 A, k1 B, k3 A; rep from * to last 4 sts, k3 B, k1 A.
Row 4: P1 A, p3 B, *p2 A, p2 B, p1 A, p5 B; rep from * to last st, p1 A.
Row 5: K1 A, *k5 B, k2 A, k2 B, k1 A; rep from * to last 4 sts, k3 B, k1 A.
Row 6: P1 A, p5 B, *p2 A, p8 B; rep from * to last 9 sts, p2 A, p6 B, p1 A.
Row 7: K1 A, k7 B, *k1 A, k9 B;

rep from * to last 7 sts, k1 A, k5 B, k1 A.
Row 8: P1 A, p4 B, *p2 A, p8 B; rep from * to last 10 sts, p2 A, p7 B, p1 A.
Row 9: K1 A, k8 B, k1 A, *k9 B, k1 A; rep from * to last 5 sts, k4 B, k1 A.
Row 10: P1 A, p1 B, *p7 A, p3 B; rep from * to last 3 sts, p3 A.
Row 11: K1 A, *k1 B, k2 A, k2 B, k5 A; rep from * to last 4 sts, k1 B, k3 A.

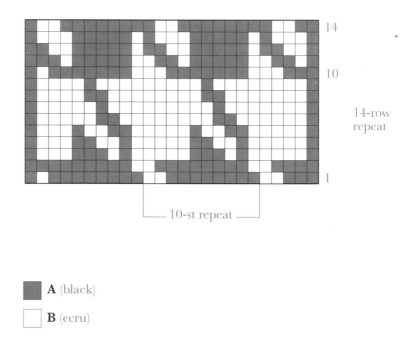

houndstooth cushion chart

Row 12: *P2 A, p2 B, p5 A, p1 B; rep from * to last 5 sts, p2 A, p2 B, p1 A.

Row 13: K1 A, *k3 B, k1 A, k1 B, k5 A; rep from * to last 4 sts, k3 B, k1 A.

Row 14: P1 A, *p2 B, p8 A; rep from * to last 4 sts, p2 B, p2 A.
Rep last 14 rows until work measures 18 in (45cm), ending with WS facing for next row.
Break off B.
P 1 row in A.
Bind off.

To make corsage

Cut a strip of fabric approximately 59 in (150cm) long and 1 in (2.5cm) wide (if necessary, piece strip by stitching flat overlapping seam). Leaving a tail approximately 8 in (20cm) long, make a "rosette" or "star" by folding strip out and back onto itself into center, holding it in place with your thumb, until six looped "points" have been folded. Secure loops at center with a stitch, and leave another tail approximately 8 in (20cm) long at back. Sew a button to center front of corsage and sew a safety pin to back.

striped cushion

To make cushion front

Using size 6 (4mm) needles and A, cast on 105 sts.
P 1 row.
Beg with a k row, work in St st and stripe patt as foll:
Row 1 (RS): K8 A, k1 B, *k7 A, k1 B; rep from * to last 8 sts, k8 A.
Row 2: P8 A, p1 B, *p7 A, p1 B; rep from * to last 8 sts, p8 A.
Rep last 2 rows until work measures 18 in (45cm), ending with WS facing for next row.
Break off B.

P 1 row in A.
Bind off.

To finish both cushions

Weave in any loose yarn ends.
Lay work out flat and gently steam.
Cut out a piece of felt 19 in (48cm) square for back of cushion.
Sew zipper in place along top of cushion, taking a ½ in (1.5cm) seam on felt and stitching close to edge on knitting; then sew other three seams.
Cut a strip of felt ½ in (1.5cm) by 9 in (23cm), fold in half lengthwise, and stitch along each long edge, close to fold and raw edges.
Trim close to stitching, and loop onto zipper puller.
Pin corsage to houndstooth cushion as shown.
Place one large button at center of each side of striped cushion and stitch them together through cushion.

69

floor cushion

A new classic—with living spaces becoming less formal, seating has taken on a softer and more casual form. Simple squares are knitted in basic stockinette stitch with super-bulky wool yarn and stitched together with visible external seams to fit over a firm foam rubber pad. A knitted button is sewn to the middle to mimic traditional upholstery.

See pages 24–25

floor cushion

materials

Any super-bulky-weight yarn, such as Rowan *Big Wool*
  Seven 3$\frac{1}{2}$ oz (100g) balls
Pair each of sizes 15 (10mm) and 11 (8mm) knitting needles
Large blunt-ended yarn needle
Satin-like lining fabric, approximately 60 in x 36 in wide (154cm x
  91cm)
Firm foam rubber cushion block, 24 in x 24 in x 4 in (61cm x
  61cm x 10cm) [h x w x d]

size

One size, approximately 24 in x 24 in (61cm x 61cm)

gauge

10 sts and 13 rows = 4 in (10cm) over St st using size 15
  (10mm) needles or size necessary to obtain gauge.

To make square panel (make 2)
Using size 15 (10mm) needles, cast
on 63 sts.
Beg with a k row, work in St st until
work measures 24 in (61cm).
Bind off.
Work another piece in same way.

To make side panel (make 4)
Using size 15 (10mm) needles, cast
on 63 sts.
Beg with a k row, work in St st until
work measures 4 in (10cm).
Bind off.
Work three more pieces in same way.

To make knitted button
Using size 11 (8mm) needles, cast
on 8 sts.
Beg with a k row, work in St st,
inc 1 st at each end of 3rd row
and then at each end of every alt
row until there are 14 sts.
Cont in St st throughout, dec 1 st at
each end of every alt row until
there are 8 sts, ending with WS
facing for next row.
P 1 row.
Bind off, leaving a long end
of yarn.
Using a blunt-ended yarn needle
and the long end of yarn, work a
running stitch all around edge of
knitting, pull up tightly, and
fasten off.

To finish
Weave in any loose yarn ends.
Lay work out flat and gently steam.
Sew top and bottom square panels
to side panels with seams on
outside, leaving a large enough
opening at one side and at top to
insert foam rubber pad.
Cover foam rubber pad with lining
fabric.
Insert covered pad into knitted
cover and sew opening closed.
Sew knitted button to center of top
of cushion with two simple stitches.

wash mitt

materials
Any double-knitting-weight hemp yarn, such as Lanaknits *Allhemp6*
   A: One $3\frac{1}{2}$ oz (100g) skein in natural
   B: One $3\frac{1}{2}$ oz (100g) skein in dark green
Pair of size 5 (3.75mm) knitting needles
Large blunt-ended yarn needle
Strip of soft suede, $\frac{5}{8}$ in (1.5cm) x 8 in (20cm) for loop
Two small mother-of-pearl buttons

size
One size—to fit average-size hand—6 in (15cm) x $8\frac{1}{4}$ in (21cm)

gauge
20 sts and 26 rows = 4 in (10cm) over St st using size 5 (3.75mm)
   needles or size necessary to obtain gauge.

pattern note
To obtain the fully-fashioned detail, work the decreases as follows:
   On a knit row: K3, k2tog, k to last 5 sts, k2tog tbl, k3.
   On a purl row: P3, p2tog tbl, p to last 5 sts, p2tog, p3.

To make wash mitt front and back (make 2)
Using size 5 (3.75mm) needles and B, cast on 32 sts.
K 2 rows (for garter st border).
Change to A and beg with a k row, work in St st for 4 in (10cm), ending with RS facing for next row.
Cont in St st throughout, inc 1 st at each end of next row—*34 sts.*

Work even until work measures $5\frac{1}{2}$ in (14cm) from cast-on edge, ending with RS facing for next row.
Dec 1 st at each end of next row and every foll 3rd row until there are 22 sts.
Work even for 1 row.
Bind off 4 sts at beg of next 4 rows.
Bind off remaining 6 sts.

To finish
Weave in any loose yarn ends.
Lay work out flat and gently steam.
Sew seam front and back together using mattress stitch and leaving border edge open for hand.
Sew one button to each side of one corner of wash mitt. Then cut a buttonhole slit at each end of suede strip and fasten it to buttons.

See pages 26–27

cable throw

A quintessentially classic throw, this piece is perfect for either a couch or a bed. Knit back and forth using a circular knitting needle in one piece with integral edges, this throw has a simple cable and rib design, which gives a refined texture. The yarn is a smooth, bulky merino wool; the result is a fluid, elegant textile to enhance any interior.

See pages 28–29

cable throw

materials

Any bulky-weight wool yarn, such as Jaeger *Extra-fine Merino Chunky*
    Thirty-six 1¾ oz (50g) balls
Size 10½ (6.5mm) circular knitting needle
Large blunt-ended yarn needle
Cable needle

size

One size, approximately 48 in x 59¾ in (122cm x 152cm)

gauge

14 sts and 20 rows = 4 in (10cm) over cable and rib stitch using size
    10½ (6.5mm) needles or size necessary to obtain gauge.

pattern note

Throw is worked in one piece back and forth in rows on a
circular needle.

To make throw

Using size 10½ (6.5mm) circular needle, cast on 202 sts.

Work in k1, p1 rib for 1½ in (4cm), ending with WS facing for next row.

Next row (WS): [Rib 28 sts, inc in next st] 6 times, rib 28 sts—*208 sts.* Cont in cable patt with 8-st k1, p1 borders as foll:

Row 1 (RS): Rib first 8 sts as set, *p3, k6, p3, k8; rep from * to last 20 sts, p3, k6, p3, rib last 8 sts as set.

Row 2: Rib first 8 sts, *k3, p6, k3, p8; rep from * to last 20 sts, k3, p6, k3, rib last 8 sts.

Row 3: Rep row 1.
Row 4: Rep row 2.
Row 5: Rep row 1.
Row 6: Rep row 2.
Row 7: Rib first 8 sts, *p3, k6, p3, slip next 4 sts onto cable needle and hold at back of work, k4, then k4 from cable needle; rep from * to last 20 sts, p3, k6, p3, rib last 8 sts.
Row 8: Rep row 2.
Row 9: Rep row 1.
Row 10: Rep row 2.
Row 11: Rep row 1.
Row 12: Rep row 2.
Rep last 12 rows until work

measures 58¼ in (148cm) from cast-on edge, ending with RS facing for next row.

Dec row (RS): [Work 28 sts in patt, k2tog] 6 times, work 28 sts in patt—*202 sts.*
Work in k1, p1 rib across all sts for 1½ in (4cm).
Bind off in rib.

To finish

Weave in any loose yarn ends.
Lay work out flat and gently steam.

stitch cushions

This wonderfully versatile cushion pattern can be worked in stockinette stitch, ribbing, or with cables. The cushion is knit in one piece with carefully positioned pattern repeats to appear seamless. The openings are fastened with large mother-of-pearl buttons, which complement the neutral palette of the natural alpaca and wool-blend yarns.

See pages 30–31

stitch cushions

materials

Any double-knitting-weight yarn, such as Rowan *RYC Baby Alpaca DK*
  Five 1¾ oz (50g) balls for each cushion
Pair each of sizes 5 (3.75mm) and 6 (4mm) knitting needles
Large blunt-ended yarn needle
Five 1 in (28mm) mother-of-pearl buttons
Pillow form to fit finished cover

size

One size, approximately 16 in x 16 in (40cm x 40cm)

gauge

22 sts and 30 rows = 4 in (10cm) over St st using size 6 (4mm) needles
  or size necessary to obtain gauge.

stitches

stockinette stitch
Row 1 (RS): K.
Row 2: P.
Rep last 2 rows to form St st.

rib pattern
Row 1 (RS): P2, *k3, p2; rep from * to end.
Row 2: K2, (p3, k2) to end.
Rep last 2 rows to form rib patt.

cable pattern

Row 1 (WS): P5, k2, p6, k2, [p8, k2, p6, k2] 4 times, p5.
Row 2: K5, [p2, k6, p2, k8] 4 times, p2, k6, p2, k5.
Row 3: Rep row 1.
Row 4: K5, [p2, slip next 3 sts onto cable needle and hold at back, k3, then k3 from cable needle, p2, k8] 4 times, p2, slip next 3 sts onto cable needle and hold at back, k3, then k3 from cable needle, p2, k5.
Rows 5–8: Rep rows 1 and 2 twice.
Rep last 8 rows to form cable patt.

To make cushion
Using size 6 (4mm) needles, cast on 87 sts.
Beg with a k row, work 10 rows in St st.
Next row (RS): Using a size 5 (3.75mm) needle, p to end (to make a neat folding row).
Change back to size 6 (4mm) needles.
Beg with a p row, work 9 rows in St st, ending with RS facing for next row.
Place a marker at each end of last row.
This completes button band.
Cable cushion only:
Inc row (RS): K9, inc in next st, [k16, inc in next st] 4 times, k9 —*92 sts.*
All cushions:
Cont in your chosen stitch patt until work measures 32 in (80cm) from markers, ending with RS facing for next row if working in St st or rib patt and WS facing for next row if working cable patt.

Cable cushion only:
Dec row (WS): P9, p2 tog, [p16, p2 tog] 4 times, p9—*87 sts.*
All cushions:
Work buttonhole band as follows: Beg a k row, work 4 rows in St st.
Buttonhole row 1 (RS): K first 6 sts, bind off next 3 sts, [k until there are 15 sts on right needle, bind off next 3 sts] 4 times, k last 5 sts.
Buttonhole row 2: P across row, casting on 3 sts over those bound off in previous row.
Work 4 rows in St st.
Next row (RS): Using a size 5 (3.75mm) needle, p to end (to make a neat folding row).
Change back to size 6 (4mm) needles.
Beg with a p row, work 3 rows in St st.
Work 2 buttonhole rows as before.
Work 4 rows in St st.
Bind off.

To finish
Weave in any loose yarn ends.
Lay work out flat and gently steam.
Fold work in half and join both side seams using mattress stitch.
Fold button and buttonhole bands in half along purl-stitch row and sew to inside.
Sew on buttons to correspond with buttonholes.
Insert pillow form.

doorstop

Often things are exactly what they are;
nothing more, nothing less. This is a
doorstop—a knitted one—filled with
pebbles. Worked in stockinette stitch from
simple parcel string, it is made in two
pieces—a triangular base and shaped top
with fully-fashioned sides—and has a
little cotton tape for a tag at the top. An
inexpensive but useful project.

See pages 32–33

doorstop

materials

Medium-weight parcel string
    Two 44 yd (40m) balls
Pair of size 7 (4.5mm) knitting needles
Large blunt-ended yarn needle
Small plastic bag
Pebbles
$3\frac{1}{2}$ in (9cm) length of cotton tape for tab, approximately $\frac{1}{2}$ in
    (1.25cm) wide

size

One size, approximately 7 in (18cm) wide at base x 9 in (23cm) tall

pattern note

To obtain the fully-fashioned detail, work the decreases as follows:
On a knit row: K2, k2tog, k to last 4 sts, k2tog tbl, k2.
On a purl row: P2, p2tog tbl, p to last 4 sts, p2tog, p2.

gauge

16 sts and 20 rows = 4 in (10cm) over St stitch using size 7
    (4.5mm) needles or size necessary to obtain gauge.

To make base

Using size 7 (4.5mm) needles, cast on 26 sts.

Beg with a k row, work in St st as foll:

Dec 1 st at each end of 3rd row and every foll 3rd row until there are 6 sts, ending with RS facing for next row.

Work even for 2 rows, ending with RS facing for next row.

Next row (RS): K1, sl 1, k2tog, psso, k2—*4 sts.*

Next row: P.

Next row: K1, sl 1, k2tog, psso—*2 sts.*

Next row: P2tog.

Fasten off.

To make top

Using size 7 (4.5mm) needles, cast on 80 sts.

Beg with a k row, work 2 rows in St st, ending with RS facing for next row.

Next row (RS): [K2, k2tog, k20, k2tog tbl] 3 times, k2—*74 sts.*

Cont in St st throughout, work even for 3 rows, ending with RS facing for next row.

Next row (RS): [K2, k2tog, k18, k2tog tbl] 3 times, k2—*68 sts.*

Work even for 3 rows, ending with RS facing for next row.

Cont to dec as set on every 4th row, working 2 sts less between decreases each time, until there are 20 sts, ending with WS facing for next row.

Work even for 3 rows, ending with RS facing for next row.

Next row (RS): [K2, k2tog, k2tog tbl] 3 times, k2—*14 sts.*

Next row: P.

Next row: [K2, k2tog tbl] 3 times, k2—*11 sts.*

Cut string, leaving a long end for seam, thread end through remaining sts, pull up tightly, and secure.

To finish

Using mattress stitch and starting at top, sew side seam on top. Sew base to top along two sides, pack a small plastic bag with pebbles, insert bag in doorstop, and sew closed along third side of base. Fold tape in half and sew tab firmly to top as shown on page 32.

lace throw

This is a fresh take on the traditional Shetland lace shawl. Although not as complex or intricate as those characteristic knits from the Scottish isles, this feminine coverlet is just as delicate. Worked in simple sections on large needles and edged in a pretty lace stitch, and made in whisper-fine kid mohair, this throw looks stunning thrown over crisp white cotton sheets.

See pages 34–35

lace throw

materials

Any fine-weight mohair yarn, such as Rowan *Kidsilk Haze*
  Ten ⅞ oz (25g) balls
Pair of size 8 (5mm) knitting needles (or size 8 (5mm) circular needle)
Medium-size blunt-ended yarn needle

size

One size, approximately 59 in x 59 in (150cm x 150cm),
  excluding edging

gauge

15 sts and 26 rows = 4 in (10cm) over St stitch using size 8 (5mm)
  needles or size necessary to obtain gauge.

pattern notes

• The throw is worked in four pieces, plus an edging.
• Cast on each piece loosely or with a size larger needle.

To make throw panels
A—Shetland lace panel
Using size 8 (5mm) needles, cast on
76 sts.
Beg with a k row, work 12 in (30cm)
in St st, ending with RS facing for
next row.
Next row(RS): K1, *yo, k2tog, k3;
rep from * to end.
Beg with a p row, work 2 rows in St st,
ending with WS facing for next row.

Cont in lace patt as foll:
Row 1 (WS): P.
Row 2: K3, *yo, k2, sl 1, k1, psso,
k2tog, k2, yo, k1; rep from * to last
st, k1.
Row 3: P.
Row 4: K2, *yo, k2, sl 1, k1, psso,
k2tog, k2, yo, k1; rep from * to last
2 sts, k2.
Rep last 4 rows until work measures
42 in (107cm) from cast-on edge.

Bind off very loosely.

B—Honeycomb lace panel
Using size 8 (5mm) needles, cast on
75 sts.
Work in lace patt as foll:
Row 1 (RS): K2, *yo, sl 1, k2tog,
psso, yo, k1; rep from * to last st, k1.
Row 2: P.
Row 3: K1, k2tog, yo, k1, *yo, sl 1,
k2tog, psso, yo, k1; rep from * to

last 3 sts, yo, sl 1, k1, psso, k1.
Row 4: P.
Rep last 4 rows until work measures
42 in (107cm).
Bind off very loosely.

C—Beginner's lace panel
Using size 8 (5mm) needles, cast on
97 sts.
Work in lace patt as foll:
Row 1 (WS) and all alt rows: P.
Rows 2, 4, and 6: K1, *yo, sl 1,
k1, psso, k1, k2tog, yo, k1; rep
from * to end.
Row 8: K2, *yo, sl 1, k2tog, psso, yo,
k3; rep from *, ending last rep k2.
Row 10: K1, *k2tog, yo, k1, yo, sl 1
k1, psso, k1; rep from * to end.
Row 12: K2tog, *yo, k3, yo, sl 1,
k2tog, psso; rep from *, ending yo,
k3, yo, sl 1, k1, psso.
Rep last 12 rows until work
measures 24 in (61cm), ending with
RS facing for next row.
Beg with a p row, cont in rev St st
until work measures 42 in (107cm)
from cast-on edge.
Bind off very loosely.

D—Diamond eyelet panel
Using size 8 (5mm) needles, cast on
89 sts.
Beg with a k row, work 2 rows in St st.
Cont in lace patt as foll:
Row 1 (RS): K3, yo, k2tog, k10,
[yo, sl 1, k1, psso, k5, k2tog, yo,
k16] twice, yo, sl 1, k1, psso, k5,
k2tog, yo, k10, k2tog, yo, k3.
Row 2: P.

Row 3: K16, [yo, sl 1, k1, psso, k3,
k2tog, yo, k18] twice, yo, sl 1, k1,
psso, k3, k2tog, yo, k16.
Row 4: P.
Row 5: K3, yo, k2tog, k12, [yo,
sl 1, k1, psso, k1, k2tog, yo, k20]
twice, yo, sl 1, k1, psso, k1, k2tog,
yo, k12, k2tog, yo, k3.
Row 6: P.
Row 7: K18, [yo, sl 1, k2tog, psso,
yo, k22] twice, yo, sl 1, k2tog, psso,
yo, k18.
Row 8: P.
Row 9: K3, yo, k2tog, k12, [k2tog,
yo, k1, yo, sl 1, k1, psso, k20] twice,
k2tog, yo, k1, yo, sl 1, k1, psso, k12,
k2tog, yo, k3.
Row 10: P.
Row 11: K16, [k2tog, yo, k3, yo,
sl 1, k1, psso, k18] twice, k2tog, yo,
k3, yo, sl 1, k1, psso, k16.
Row 12: P.
Row 13: K3, yo, k2tog, k10,
[k2tog, yo, k5, yo, sl 1, k1, psso,
k16] twice, k2tog, yo, k5, yo, sl 1,
k1, psso, k10, k2tog, yo, k3.
Row 14: P.
Row 15: K14, [k2tog, yo, k7, yo,
sl 1, k1, psso, k14] 3 times.
Row 16: P.
Rep last 16 rows until work
measures 59 in (150cm).
Bind off very loosely.

E—Lace edging
Using size 8 (5mm) needles, cast on
7 sts.
Row 1: [Yo, k2tog] twice, yo, p3.
Row 2: P4, yo, p2tog, yo, p2.

Row 3: [Yo, k2tog] twice, yo, p5.
Row 4: P6, yo, p2tog, yo, p2.
Row 5: [Yo, k2tog] twice, yo, p7.
Row 6: P8, yo, p2tog, yo, p2.
Row 7: [Yo, k2tog] twice, yo, p9.
Row 8: P7, [p2tog, yo] twice,
p2tog, p1.
Row 9: Yo, k3tog, [yo, k2tog]
twice, p6.
Row 10: P5, [p2tog, yo] twice,
p2tog, p1.
Row 11: Yo, k3tog, [yo, k2tog]
twice, p4.
Row 12: P3, p2tog, [yo, p2tog]
twice, p1.
Row 13: Yo, k3tog, [yo, k2tog]
twice, p2.
Row 14: P1, p2tog, [yo, p2tog]
twice, p1.
Rep last 14 rows until edging
measures 8¼ yd (7.5m).
Bind off.

To finish
Weave in any loose yarn ends.
Lay panels out flat. With bound-off
ends aligned side by side, sew panels
A and B together along selvages,
using mattress stitch, but keeping a
"light touch" as fabric is so airy;
then join panels B and C together
also along selvages. Finally, sew
panel D along one selvage to bound-
off edges of other three panels A,
B, and C. Pin and stitch edging E
in place around throw, making a
full gather at each corner—working
along one section at a time makes it
easier. Gently steam.

beaded cushion

This cushion is essentially basic, yet its embellishments make it quietly feminine. Knitted in pure linen and worked in stockinette stitch, it couldn't be easier to make. The motif is cut from a printed linen fabric, hand stitched to the knitting, and then embellished with small wooden beads for added impact.

See pages 36–37

beaded cushion

materials

Any double-knitting-weight hemp yarn, such as Lanaknits *Allhemp6*
   Three 1¾ oz (50g) balls
Pair of size 7 (4.5mm) knitting needles
Large blunt-ended yarn needle
Approximately 100 small wooden beads
Approximately ½ yd (0.5m) of natural linen fabric for backing
Approximately 44 in (112cm) of narrow cotton tape for ties
Pillow form to fit finished cover
Small piece of printed fabric, such as cotton or linen, with a large
   floral motif for appliqué
Sheet of appliqué bonding web adhesive
Sewing needle and thread

size

One size, approximately 16 in x 16 in (40cm x 40cm)

gauge

18½ sts and 24 rows = 4 in (10cm) over St st using size 7 (4.5mm)
   needles or size necessary to obtain gauge.

To make cushion front

Using size 7 (4.5mm) needles, cast on
76 sts.

Beg with a k row, work in St st for
16 in (40cm).

Bind off.

Appliqué and beading

Take fabric with large floral motif
and cut around motif, leaving
narrow border.

Press appliqué onto cushion front
using appliqué bonding web
adhesive.

Hand stitch around motif outline
and along details inside motif, such
as petal outlines and leaf veins.

Further embellish with beads to
enhance motif.

To finish

Weave in any loose ends on
knitting, then lay out flat and
gently steam.

Cushion back

Cut two pieces of fabric, each
$12\frac{1}{2}$ in x 17 in (32.5cm x 43cm).
Along one long edge of each
piece fold $\frac{1}{2}$ in (1.5cm) to wrong
side twice and stitch to form a
double hem.

Lay knitting right-side up and place
both back pieces wrong-side down
on top, so that raw edges of fabric
extend $\frac{1}{2}$ in (1.5cm) past edges of
knitting and hemmed edges overlap
at center.

Pin and stitch around all sides,
taking a $\frac{1}{2}$ in (1.5cm) seam on

fabric and stitching close to edge
on knitting.

Turn right-side out.

Cotton-tape ties

Cut cotton tape into four pieces,
each 11 in (28cm) long—two for
each side of back opening. Hem
one end of each piece, then fold
hem at other end and sew this end
to cushion back with a cross-stitch,
positioning each pair of ties about
8 in (20cm) apart at center of back
opening.

Insert pillow form and tie tapes
into bows.

patchwork throw

A simple motif using both knitting and fabric make this throw a unique variation on the traditional patchwork quilt. Rustic nep yarns and textural fabrics— such as tweed, flannel, and herringbone —in tones of wheat, stone, and stormy gray are patched together and backed with contrasting corduroy. Made in five different textural stitches, the knitted pieces could be used to make up the entire throw if preferred.

See pages 38–39

patchwork throw

materials

Any aran-weight wool yarn, such as Rowan *Scottish Tweed Aran*

 A: One 3½ oz (100g) ball light gray

 B: One 3½ oz (100g) ball dark gray

 C: One 3½ oz (100g) ball beige

 D: One 3½ oz (100g) ball ecru

Pair of size 8 (5mm) knitting needles

Cable needle

Large blunt-ended yarn needle

Assorted fabrics (and matching thread) for patchwork in six different textures and/or colors

 E: beige herringbone

 F: black and white herringbone

 G: black flannel

 H: gray flannel

 I: woven beige

 J: woven black

1¾ yd (1.5m) of corduroy (59in (150cm) wide) for backing

Microfilament sewing thread

size

One size, approximately 45¾ in x 45¾ in (116cm x 116cm)

gauge

20 sts and 24 rows = 4 in (10cm) over St st using size 8 (5mm) needles or size necessary to obtain gauge.

pattern notes

- A total of 20 knitted whole hexagons and 2 half-hexagons are required to make the throw. The knitted hexagons measure 7 in x 7 in (18cm x 18cm). When cutting out the fabric hexagons, cut approximately 36 to allow for making the edging pieces. For the fabric hexagons, cut to the same size as the knitted hexagons but add a ¾ in (2cm) seam allowance all around the edge.
- To create a neat edge when knitting the hexagons, always increase or decrease one stitch in from the side edges.

To make knitted hexagons

Using size 8 (5mm) needles, cast on 16 sts.

Work first 2 rows of chosen stitch patt, ending with RS facing for next row. Keeping chosen stitch patt correct throughout and working inc sts in stitch patt (unless stated otherwise), inc 1 st at each end of next row and then at each end of every foll 3rd row until there are 30 sts. Work even for 2 rows.

Half hexagon only:
Work even for 2 rows more.
Bind off.

Full hexagon only:
Dec 1 st at each end of next row and then at each end of every foll 3rd row until there are 16 sts. Work even for 1 row.
Bind off—*43 rows in total.*

Stitch patterns

Follow instructions for knitted hexagons while working one of following stitch patterns. Sample each stitch pattern to familiarize yourself with increases/decreases. Work inc sts in individual stitch patterns except where stated otherwise.

Double moss stitch

Make one hexagon in each of A, C, and D, plus one half hexagon in B.
Worked across a multiple of 4 sts.
Row 1 (RS): *K2, p2; rep from * to end.
Row 2: Rep row 1.
Rows 3 and 4: *P2, k2; rep from * to end.
Rep last 4 rows to form double moss st.

Basket stitch

Make one hexagon in each of A, B, C, and D.
Worked across a 16-st panel.
Work inc sts in garter st.
Row 1 (RS): K.
Row 2: P.
Row 3: K2, [k1, p4, k1] twice, k2.
Row 4: K2, [p1, k4, p1] twice, k2.
Rows 5 and 6: Rep rows 3 and 4.
Rows 7 and 8: Rep rows 1 and 2.
Row 9: K2, [p2, k2, p2] twice, k2.
Row 10: K2, [k2, p2, k2] twice, k2.
Rows 11 and 12: Rep rows 9 and 10.
Rep last 12 rows to form patt.

Reverse cable rib

Make one hexagon in each of A, B, C and D.
Worked across a 16-st panel.

Work inc sts in St st.

Row 1 (RS): K1, p3, k8, p3, k1.

Row 2: P1, k3, p8, k3, p1.

Rows 3 and 4: Rep rows 1 and 2.

Row 5: K1, p3, slip next 2 sts onto cable needle and leave at back of work, k2, k2 from cable needle, slip next 2 sts onto cable needle and leave at front of work, k2, k2 from cable needle, p3, k1.

Row 6: Rep row 2.

Rep last 6 rows to form patt.

Seed stitch rib

Make one hexagon in each of B, C, and D, plus one half hexagon in A.

Worked across a multiple of 4 sts.

Row 1: *K3, p1; rep from * to end.

Row 2: *K2, p1, k1; rep from * to end.

Rep last 2 rows to form patt.

Seed stitch stripe

Make one hexagon in each of B, C, and D.

Beg with a RS row, work 4 rows in seed stitch, ending with RS facing for next row.

Beg with a k row, work 4 rows in St st.

Rep last 8 rows to form patt.

Stockinette stitch/garter stitch stripe

Make one hexagon in each of A, B, and D.

K 7 rows.

**P 1 row.

K 1 row.

P 1 row.

K 9 rows.**

Rep from ** to ** twice more.

To finish

Cut about 36 fabric hexagons from assorted fabrics (see pattern notes on page 99).

Patch arrangement

Lay out fabric and knitted hexagons, following diagram on page 101 for knitted hexagons, distributing fabric pieces evenly.

Make a chart of your final arrangement, numbering each hexagon, then pin a label to each hexagon to match your chart.

Patchwork seams

Hand sew each diagonal row of knitted hexagons together, and machine stitch each diagonal row of fabric hexagons together, including partial hexagons at ends of diagonal rows.

Pin knitted rows of hexagons on top of seam allowances of rows of fabric hexagons, aligning knitted edge with seam line on fabric hexagons. Baste in place and remove pins. Baste partial fabric hexagons in place at ends of knitted rows.

Using microfilament thread, machine zigzag rows together along knitted edges.

Patchwork backing

Gently press patchwork and place on top of backing, with wrong sides together. Sew patchwork to backing around edge and trim off any excess backing around edge.

Edging

Cut four edging strips from fabric, each 2¾ in (7.5cm) wide and length of throw plus ½ in (1.5cm) hem allowance at each end of strip. Machine stitch a strip to two opposite edges of patchwork, with RS together and taking a ¾ in (2cm) seam. Turn edging to back, fold under ½ in (1.5cm), and hand sew in place.

Sew on other two strips in same way, folding in ends at corner edges.

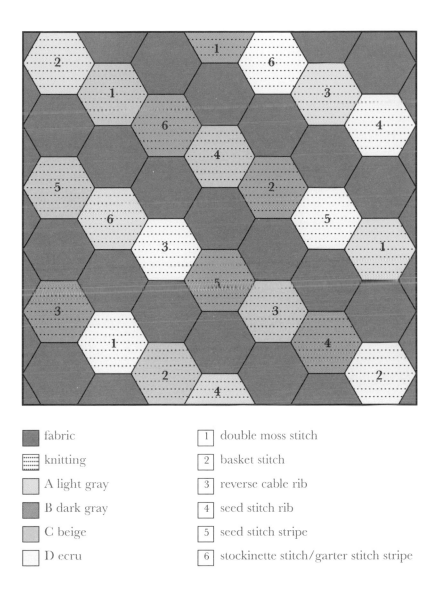

■	fabric	1 double moss stitch
▦	knitting	2 basket stitch
□	A light gray	3 reverse cable rib
■	B dark gray	4 seed stitch rib
■	C beige	5 seed stitch stripe
□	D ecru	6 stockinette stitch/garter stitch stripe

yarns

Although I have recommended a specific yarn for the projects in the book, you can use substitutes if you like. A description of each of the yarns used is given below.

If you decide to use an alternative yarn, purchase a substitute that is as close as possible to the original in thickness, weight, and texture so that it will work with the pattern instructions. Buy only one ball to start with, so you can test the effect. Calculate the number of balls you will need by yards/meters rather than by weight. The recommended knitting-needle size and knitting gauge on the yarn labels are extra guides to the yarn thickness.

To obtain Debbie Bliss, Lanaknits, or Rowan (and Jaeger) yarns, go to the websites below to find a store in your area:

www.debbieblissonline.com for Debbie Bliss
www.hempforknitting.com for Lanaknits
www.knitrowan.com for Rowan

Debbie Bliss *Cashmerino Aran*
An aran-weight wool-blend yarn
Recommended knitting-needle size: size 8 (5mm)
Gauge: 18 sts and 24 rows = 4 in (10cm) over St st
Ball size: 98 yds (90m) per $1^3/_4$ oz (50g) ball
Yarn specification: 55% merino wool, 33% microfiber, 12% cashmere

Debbie Bliss *Cashmerino Superchunky*
A super-bulky-weight wool-blend yarn
Recommended knitting-needle size: size 11 (7.5mm)
Gauge: 12 sts and 17 rows = 4 in (10cm) over St st
Ball size: 82 yds (75m) per $3^1/_2$ oz (50g) ball
Yarn specification: 55% merino wool, 33% microfiber, 12% cashmere

Lanaknits *Allhemp6*
A double-knitting-weight hemp yarn
Recommended knitting-needle size: size 5 (3.75mm)
Gauge: 22 sts and 28 rows = 4 in (10cm) over knitted St st
Skein size: 165 yds (150m) per $3^1/_2$ oz (100g) skein
Yarn specification: 100% hemp

Lanaknits *Hemp Natural Hemp6*
A double-knitting-weight hemp yarn
Recommended knitting-needle size: size 5 (3.75mm)
Gauge: 22 sts and 28 rows = 4 in (10cm) over knitted St st
Cone size: 850 yds (775m) per 18 oz (500g) cone
Yarn specification: 100% hemp

Jaeger *Extra-fine Merino Chunky*
A bulky-weight wool-blend yarn
Recommended knitting-needle size: size 10 (6mm)
Gauge: 15 sts and 20 rows = 4 in (10cm) over St st
Ball size: 69 yds (63m) per $1^3/_4$ oz (50g) ball
Yarn specification: 100% merino wool

Rowan *Big Wool*
A super-bulky-weight wool yarn
Recommended knitting-needle size: size 15 or 19 (10mm or 15mm)
Gauge: 7–9 sts and 10–$12^1/_2$ rows = 4 in (10cm) over St st
Ball size: 87 yds (80m) per $3^1/_2$ oz (100g) ball
Yarn specification: 100% merino wool

Rowan *Cotton Glacé*
A fine-weight cotton yarn
Recommended knitting-needle size: sizes 3–5 (3.25–3.75mm)
Gauge: 23 sts and 32 rows = 4 in (10cm) over St st
Ball size: 126 yds (115m) per $1^3/_4$ oz (500g) ball
Yarn specification: 100% cotton

Rowan *Kidsilk Haze*

A fine-weight mohair-blend yarn

Recommended knitting-needle size: sizes 3–8 (3.25–5mm)

Gauge: 18–25 sts and 23–24 rows = 4 in (10cm) over St st

Ball size: 230 yds (210m) per $^7/_8$ oz (25g) ball

Yarn specification: 70% super kid mohair, 30% silk

Rowan *RYC Baby Alpaca DK*

A double-knitting-weight wool yarn

Recommended knitting-needle size: size 6 (4mm)

Gauge: 22 sts and 30 rows = 4 in (10cm) over St st

Ball size: 109 yds (100m) per $1^3/_4$ oz (50g) ball

Yarn specification: 100% alpaca

Rowan *RYC Cashsoft DK*

A double-knitting-weight wool-blend yarn

Recommended knitting-needle size: size 6 (4mm)

Gauge: 22 sts and 30 rows = 4 in (10cm) over St st

Ball size: 142 yds (130m) per $1^3/_4$ oz (50g) ball

Yarn specification: 57% fine merino wool, 33% microfiber, 10% cashmere

Rowan *Scottish Tweed Aran*

An aran-weight wool yarn

Recommended knitting-needle size: sizes 8–9 (5–5.5mm)

Gauge: 16 sts and 23 rows = 4 in (10cm) over St st

Ball size: 186 yds (170m) per $3^1/_2$ oz (100g) ball

Yarn specification: 100% wool

Rowan *Scottish Tweed Chunky*

A bulky weight wool yarn

Recommended knitting-needle size: size 11 (7.5mm)

Gauge: 12 sts and 16 rows = 4 in (10cm) over St st

Ball size: 109 yds (100m) per $3^1/_2$ oz (100g) ball

Yarn specification: 100% wool

abbreviations

beg	begin(ning)
cm	centimeter(s)
cont	continu(e)(ing)
dec	decreas(e)(ing)
garter st	garter stitch (k every row)
foll	follow(s)(ing)
g	gram(s)
inc	increas(e)(ing)
k	knit
m	meter(s)
M1	make one stitch by picking up horizontal loop before next stitch and working into back of it
mm	millimeter(s)
p	purl
patt	pattern; work in pattern
psso	pass slipped stitch over
rep	repeat
rev St st	reverse stockinette stitch (p all RS rows, k all WS rows)
RS	right side(s)
sl	slip
st(s)	stitch(es)
St st	stockinette stitch (k all RS rows, p all WS rows)
tog	together
WS	wrong side(s)
tbl	through back of loop(s)
yo	yarn over (yarn over right needle to make a new stitch)

[ ] * Repeat instructions between brackets, or after or between asterisks, as many times as instructed.

acknowledgments

My personal thanks and appreciation just have to go to the exceptional people who have collaborated to create this book.

It is a priviledge to work with Quadrille Publishing, a publisher of style and insight, who consistently push the boundary. Alison Cathie for her exciting company and team, most especially my Editorial Director and mentor Jane O'Shea, whose vision, encouragement, and style have nurtured my career as an author. Creative Director Helen Lewis, for her exacting innovation for each new project. Lisa Pendreigh, project manager, whose rigorous support and inimitable professionalism is without equal and Claire Peters who has brought a new vitality to the design.

It has been simply fantastic to have Katya de Grunwald photograph this collection; her exceptional and distinctive vision, together with Beth Dadswell's unique and inspirational styling, continually surprise, delight, and surpass all my expectations.

My immense appreciation goes to Sally Lee for her contribution; my amazing creative practitioner for her ready support, enthusiasm, expertise, and friendship. To Mary Potter and Christine Dilley for their superb work, and also Hilary Jagger, a craft designer of rare and exceptional caliber. My heartfelt thanks to Rosy Tucker; her diligence and meticulous hard work in checking all the patterns is invaluable.

Special thanks to Stephen Sheard of Coats Craft UK, as well as Kate Buller and the team at Rowan Yarns. Tony Brooks of Yeoman Yarns, Debbie Bliss and Designer Yarns, and Lana Hames of Lanaknits for primarily creating yarns of the highest quality but invaluably for their generosity in contributing both yarns and enthusiastic support for this project.

Finally, this book is dedicated to the "creative spirit"—that power that makes us go beyond the ordinary, the purely practical, to adorn and decorate and make something our own.